I Call Upon
the Witches

poems by
Chloe Hanks

"A sinner could repent, be absolved of his sin, and rejoin the parish. A witch could not." — Stacey Schiff (The Witches: Salem, a history, 2015)

In memory of Petronella de Meath, 1300-1324, executed as an accomplice to suspected witch Alice Kyteller, and the first to be burnt at the stake in Great Britain. Kyteller herself escaped execution for the crime of heresy.

Contents

Acknowledgements

About the Author

About the Publisher

Foreword

In the early stages of writing this project, I sat with my dissertation supervisor, Dr Jack McGowan, and explained that if asked to write a story about a witch, a group of writers would each articulate a very different image and character profile. Historian Suzannah Lipscomb discusses this in her study, *Witchcraft: A Ladybird Expert Book*, by commenting how she was "haunted" by Roald Dahl's *Grand High Witch*. Similarly, my own fixation with witches began with Jill Murphy's *The Worst Witch*.** Whilst these are two very contrasting contemporary characterizations, both echo aspects of what we might attribute to the archetype.

This archetype alludes to what some might consider stereotypically witchy. We all recognize the Wicked Witch of the West, although I might be alone in my secret love for her. What is clear from dissecting each of these characterizations whilst observing the historical context they emerged from is that female villains have very much been limited to these archetypes. With the execution of thousands of skilled women in the Early Modern period, the label of 'witch' was used to belittle their identities, undermine their craft and pose upon them a death sentence. In their place took forth an evolution of speculative literature. What might these so-called witches look like: these images of ugly, often childless women who dare to dabble in rituals and herbal remedies are a reflection cast by the patriarchal lens through which literature has been observed.

This is changing. We are beginning to acknowledge

---

*   Suzannah Lipscomb, Witchcraft: A Ladybird Expert Book, (London: Penguin Random House UK, 2018) p. 2

**   Jill Murphy, The Worst Witch, (London: Penguin, 2011)

witchcraft as a legitimate Wiccan practice rather than a supernatural exhaust of evil. We are beginning to celebrate women and their rights to be powerful, or childless, or successful, or even isolate. We are beginning to characterize women as more than just good, or kind, or pretty. And through this, we are beginning to do justice to our female villains and their right to be challenging and complex and sometimes unpleasant. To do this is to accept women in their authenticity and their imperfections: we all have as much villainy in us as we do main character moments.

By the end of writing this book, I was content in its movement through the evolution of the witch in literature; each poem is written in response to an archetype that comprises her character development. In its completion, this book gathers the fictional witches and pays tribute to them. In this, the collection also pulls focus to the [estimated] 50,000 people who have been executed under the weaponized label of 'witch;' and, it settles into a moment that breathes life into the authenticity of what it truly is to be a witch. Which, to me, in conjunction with the practice, *is to be a person at peace with the authenticity of oneself in spite of all else.*

I hope you enjoy these poems. I hope you find something here that makes you view witches in a different light, and I hope a fragment of the history, however far removed from emerald skin and broomsticks, enlightens you as it did so me.

— Chloe Hanks, *January 2022*

A Spell to Grow a Witch;

*(you will need: pumpkin seeds,
deprived of sunlight for 24 hours or more)*

When moonlight steals the sky so black
we grow witches from pumpkin seeds;
the devil takes his spirits back
when moonlight steals the sky so black.
A witch's magic keeps on track,
with no refrain from wicked deeds—
when moonlight steals the sky so black
we grow witches from pumpkin seeds.

Blood Letting*

Burn thee, this clay
figure—clad
with fingers that point.
Caricatures the witches shaped
with their numbed fingerprints,
pin pricked; limbs distorted.

Old Demdike hanged
from a branch that night
like an echo of what was
to come, what happenstance
would bring forth these
women to me like mothers.

These are not my women
pressed into their finery,
sugared lips and protestant
hips. No—

these are my women—
clawing back their femininity
with a clay doll, shaped to
an enemy.

----

*   Elizabeth Southerns, also known as Demdike,
confessed to the crime of Witchcraft and was a key figure in
the Pendle Witch Trials.

Joan*

Stones crumble in their numbers,
sand for every witch lost with no name;
no defining conclusion, just flame—

dancing like dust on the wind just the same,
lost in a current like breeze, swiftly eloping,
drawing the men to their knees.

Stray against any finite ending,
names often force themselves back into life—
drawing blood from aged wounds,

closure is a modern concept, like a witch
emerging to retaliate. No defining solution,
no solace in a name; just flame.

---

*   Joan of Arc was burned at the stake in 1431. Found guilty on a plethora of charges, her legacy and symbolic death have often led to rumours of witchcraft.

Tituba's Cauldron

Stand before the smoking mirror,
dressed head to toe in cascading silk

as dismal as the charcoal that became
their bones when the men smoked them—

as dark as the magic you pooled from
your hand. The cauldron smoulders

like an alchemist's set, aglow in shades
of dazzling green. You watch the magic

translucent through the glass panel;
you watch yourself as though you are

the epitome of sorcery. This cauldron
is not yours. Your pale skin tinges emerald

and the irony in your greenery is not lost.
You pour the witchcraft from your fingertips

but their names are lost on your lips; as though
all you can bring yourself to utter is the spell.

All of these shackled witches should be
your women as well—

maleficium is a learned tool.
Let the mother speak to you.

This cauldron is shaped like a hexagon,
you've been hexing the men like the queen

of the Amazons. Shed your cloak and face the magic.
Earn your place before you earn your facet.

You select your ladle and pour your concoction,
drinking it down. This initiation breaks you down,

it tastes like witchcraft now. And the smoking mirror,
there to poise all truth, simply cannot take her eyes off
of you.

And when you pause to take a look, you see through—
you are green with envy and green with truth.

This witch chose her women selectively
and used the name to break her fall.

Emerald fingers caress unfamiliar skin—
let us begin, how long before it all sinks in.

Some girls are not there for her women,
and the witches know what to do

with a villain.

The Testament of Petronella·

Familiar, you speak to her through me
as moonlight floods our meeting place with light
our sister begs a fate she won't foresee.
I am the witch they'll burn to death that night.

You have such secrets she has not foretold
and in her faith in us I am now doomed.
But I will serve Alice and meet my grave,
and what, dear friend, will then become of you?

Familiar, you have a godly form.
Her name will be preserved on every page,
the men will come to drag me from my bed—
my death upon the stake will be their stage.

Our Alice will escape her timely death
and skulk away, devil between her legs.

---

*   Petronella de Meath was the maid servant of Dame
Alice Kyteller. When the latter fled the country from charges
of heresy, Petronella was executed as an accomplice to
witchcraft.

Call Me Witch

I have sheltered my closet bones
as though love itself was a plague.
Gathering my twig, twine friends
late into the night as echoes call me witch.

I have peered into forest fairy gatherings,
danced alone to the great wolf's howl-
I have dared to wander without chaperone
as great men call me witch.

I have dressed my sacred skin in
red garments, both lace and silk;
I have let strange fingers unpick
the stitches as they laugh and call me witch.

I have taken my twig, twine treasures
and followed my faithful forest path.
Here I have built my own empire of fire
as men and wives gather to burn the witch.

The Hanging Tree

Let us walk down to the river
near the old hanging tree
where we shall gather once again
to hang a witch or three.
We stand before the forest brow,
the night a dazzling glow.
From here we trace the path of thieves—
where all the witches go.

As air falls still and stagnant dreams
collectively turn cold,
we'll meet beneath the hanging tree
to greet witches of old.
The echo of their whispers soft
the sun not long has set.
Tonight, we cross the breach of ghosts
a brand-new soul to let.

I'm in my favourite Sunday dress,
you're dressed in earthly green-
we let the river guide us there
to stand before the tree.
And soon we're not the only ones
that delve into the night;
we cluster like a band of thieves
to claim this ghastly sight.

There's apple blossom dripping down,
in poison to the tips
I've walked along this path before
to one more feared than this.
And so, we witches meet the hunt;

our pivotal disguise— ·
from here we must disperse, my dear
to meet not earthly eyes.

I look upon this mortal's face;
she echoes what could be.
What devils could have brought her here
to dangle from a tree?
Her hair hangs dry like wildflowers,
her eyes could stop the sun.
She found herself the people's hunt
the most desired one.

The full moon light now takes its time
in keeping with the night,
a hangman's noose, a burning cross:
our only source of light.
Suspended like the autumn leaves
just hanging by a thread;
we kiss the ground she walked upon
for now, this makes her bed.

There's silence by the riverbank
near the old hanging tree-
an eerie creak, decaying rope,
the witchy air we breathe.
We say a prayer for witches lost
their names I daren't speak-
they'll find me by the hanging tree,
our secret so to keep.

Such secrets loom above the trees,
in darkness with the moon.
The time has come to leave again
we'll meet our sisters soon.

With tilted heads towards the sky
we wander through the trees.
We gathered on the darkest night
to hang a witch or three.

There's comfort in the forest
for here we take our leave.
I call upon the witches
and so, they come to me.

Call on Twilight

it pins you down

where are your comrades now?
is there an aching in your groin

where you thought she should be
but she won't be.
not ever,
not now—

your blood stains the incantation bowl,
she lapped each drop with a serpent's tongue.

she traced your body with your own
superficial wand. spread her poison through

your lust. you never should have pinned
her down. you belong to the witches now.

Snow Queen

She pulsates, the magic pooling at her feet.
Erupting in such cacophony, her decibels
have the animals fleeing far, far away—

like a scene from a biblical film, her limbs glow
with this perishable incantation. If magic were
a being you could dazzle into bed, it would be her.

Her eyes remain guileless, a futile display of faith
in this brand-new feeling; drinking in the wildness.
Part of her still yearns for the erosion of a sunglow.

Skin bitten and dazzling, always—
part of her wonders if that is what it felt like to kiss her;
always floating off elsewhere, fragmenting like a frozen
river,
thawed against the bite of Winter.

Hagley

They found a witch in Hagley wood,
where no one ever thought they would.
They say such women gathered here
to kneel before the Wych Elm.

They found her in the palest moon,
she had no cloak, she had no broom—
she barely held an emerald glow
there knelt before the Wych Elm.

They found this witch among the trees
though no one can explain to me
how a Witch's carcass came to be
stuffed safe inside the Wych Elm.

Swim the Witch

In hostile winds, these natures chill my bones
as murky waters ebb and bob and flow.
The devils of this world make themselves known
to send me down to where the lost things go.

Beneath my feet, the bridge begins to shake;
the tremble of the water's open arms.
And brittle though my bones may bend and break
the ripples form, both tentative and calm.

May devils be tormented by the sound
of bodies greeting water down below—
as corpses are united with the ground,
I stand upon this bridge and ache to know:

what idle force could ever cheer for this?
to stand and sing, 'it's time to swim the witch.'

Your Tinder Match is a Witch

Now bloody your fists
and have me for the taking
you wouldn't believe
how my bones have been breaking;
I'm drawn to the cusp
and my fingers are bleeding
and who would have thought
that it's you I'd be needing.
I've fought off the demons
they'll leave us tonight
but we don't have much time
and I need you for life.
If we get the spell wrong
I'll be shattered forever
and I don't see a way
things could get any better.
I know that you're scared
and you think I'm a stranger;
if you don't trust my magic
just feed off the danger—

Oh, don't mind my friend,
he's been sat there for months;
just the bones of a man
that I failed to love once.

The Four Witches

An engraving on Paper attributed to Albrecht Durer

A black rose blooms in shadows cast
by waking moons – devils delight
as four women gather to form
a coven bathed in candlelight.

Each one shakes off her fabric skin
and sacred circles take their shape;
they revel in their womanhood,
while devils pick a soul to take.

Familiars creep to the scene
as rose petals form fleeting ghosts—
the four witches stand hand in hand
to meet the one to be his host.

The witches suckle hungry imps –
they settle to a mortal frame,
while devils gift the magic to
both witches and puckles the same.

Black roses bloom to bring the thorn;
but only once the curse is sworn.

Oh, To Love Her

To love her is to love
blindly— sacrificial lambs
discarded to a cavernous pit,
emerging blood stained and bruised.

To love her is to be your own.
A moment you share with her, the
next she's gone. Forgiveness
begins to roll off the tongue.

To love her is to love and never love again,
when love equates to pain. When love begins
to eat and eat away.

To love her is to carry weight
until your bones fragment and break.
Shackled into shape—
push the Witch away.

To love her is to love the way
she blinks each tear to the cusp;
blood spills like a devil's blush,
bodies discarded to rust.

To love her is to tolerate every drip of poison
she cultivates into a home cooked meal.
Head on her shoulder, playing wife
and playing lover.

Soul dancing with another,
Ghosts emerging for the rapture.

Love Potion

Only a fool would take a witch to bed
and cradle her beneath a harvest moon;
if only you could see inside her head.

You hang on each forbidden word she says;
as night falls still, you sneak into her room.
Only a fool would take a witch to bed.

With silent spells she has you blushing red
and you've been singing such romantic tunes,
If only you could see inside her head.

You're leaving magic footprints as you tread
bare foot to sit and ride upon her broom.
Only a fool would take a witch to bed.

You sacrifice your bones to bake her bread
and let her leave your haven much too soon,
if only you could see inside her head.

She would prefer to love devils instead;
she may not always come back home to you.
Only a fool would take a witch to bed—
if only you could see inside her head.

The Witches Wear Red

Bring me out of the shadows,
dress me in your cloak—
have me cradle the demons
you've danced with the most.
Kiss the dirt pressed in gently
to the souls of my feet,
find the fiercest of witches
and bring them to me.
As the sharp moon has risen,
we seek out the dark;
bleeding light like a dagger
dug straight through my heart.
And if women are witches,
like Tituba said,
don't ever forget that
the witches wear red.

A beacon is lost when
such grand witches die,
and for women like this
I would lay down my life.
I call upon witches
to see through the night,
I call upon devils
to set us alight—
to glow like the embers
such hungry men fed,
and don't ever forget that
the witches wear red.

The Witch's House

The witch hides; her house aglow
with moonlight bouncing off a rim
of Poison Ivy – this, her spellcaster, her
devil's gift, acts as a lighthouse for
those bearing the weight of a curse.

The eleventh hour birthed an
extravagant plot. The witch's acute hearing
selects the correct knock, knock, knock—
the girl enters, cloaked in her intimacy,
to deliver the gift upon the kitchen table.

The witch has brewed her magic;
the shade of healing. She braces the girl
as a devil should. Blood drips down upon
the sharpened tools and settles in a
sacred circle upon the witch's carpet.

Witches could deliver us pathetic
fallacy, quite easily; but the clouds
hold in their treasures as the fever
begins to burn— the air outside
as stagnant as an empty womb.

The witch buries her blood soaked
tablecloth. The witch burns a fire
to sterilize the tools. The witch
wipes the blood from her apothecary
stool. The girl slumbers with dreams

of blood-soaked clouds, of shapes
that bleed out into a nightmare—

waking with sweat in her hair,
looking around into a devil's stare
as she reaches her fingers to
meet the blood down there.

Paddleboards*

It is the month the leaves catch alight
and the grass crunches beneath their feet
as the witches take their paddleboards to the river.
They behave like caricatures, a fragment of
delightful fiction. The dolls take to the river
like baby ducklings on a springtime pond—

they speak to the darling creatures of the water.
They float like crows on air; puckles dancing upon
the face of a stream. A single one may do no harm
but in their hundreds, they pose a delicate threat.
Nothing makes the lions shudder quite like a murder
of crows dancing the steps of their womanhood.

Each little one stands tall on a tentative balance,
ankles bracing the pressure of the elements, ice
water groans for a witch's embrace. Stronger together,
they cluster, as the paddle-boarding witches cross
the breach of the river. Aching in the bones of a
waking October— brightness meets their mother.

It is quiet in the oneness of their giggles. Other
to the forces that watch, the onlookers. Sweeping
across the skyline, spotted by birdwatchers and news
hunters alike. No one can touch our witches now.
The hunters would tremble in their slumbers if they
could see the spectacle. The witches and their
gatherings.

---

*   In the Autumn months, hundreds of people dressed
as witches take to the Willamette river to paddleboard.

The Night Witches*

They take the lunar moment
to dance— free and dispersing like
stars. Illuminated and infinite.

The noise, the nightmarish gore
of a sky full of witches. Night witches;
bringers of fire and blood.

Gifts from the moon—
fear the night-time glow; for
it burns bright orange and screams.

Eclipsing the glow with a
jagged silhouette, they forge monsters
from their great iron broomsticks.

---

*　　The nickname attributed to a band of female aviators
that made up the WWII, German 588th Night Bomber
Regiment.

Maleficium

Teach me the songs of the Sea Witch
and I'll serenade you to a slumber,
as the gentle waves submerge you below –

I could learn the words of ancient craft;
sorcery and spirits. You'll wake in the night
to find empty rooms that spill with invisible things.

I'll reside like a house witch – in my own
refuge I discover solitude. I'll nurture you
as night falls, soft and slow across this shared horizon.

As I dabble with potion and practice,
finding friends in the fires and comfort on the hearth –
brew the magick with me.

I too have raged wars by mistaken identity –
I fled from view; cloaked in wickedness. I'll
exchange my emerald skin for herbal remedy.

I shall shed my skin like The Four Witches;
laid bare in my craft – trust no woman whose
shape becomes her weapon.

I could stand tall like Correllian – revel in
my newfound passion and I'll lead the
masses. As eternal covens form,

I'll wake against the plague of the others
while they suppress our magic with mortal food
and diminish our bones beneath the feet of horses.

I find my coven strong; maiden, mother
and crone. Sleep with me and cast with me
my witches – together strong.

Black Magic

for Lydia, Lydia & Ray

His love pulled the music from me
as easily as the witches fed me black magic—

as though devils lurked in every audience
I ever sang for, always chanting for more.

Who wouldn't feed off of magic like that?
his love set the melodies alight,

he couldn't bear it, to hear me lost in the art
I made from the boys who came before him.

That's the thing about devils, they get so
painfully jealous and before you know it

you're lacing their chai tea with poison leaves
just to find yourself a minute to breathe—

fleeting moments where the witches would
come to me. Their fingers would lace into mine

whilst we waited until the moon was high
and each witch would take their time to hold

me, breathe me back to life. Was it music
or magic or something else— his love pulled

the music from me as easily as the witches fed me
black magic. Drawing beauty from something

tragic; discarding devils to the wind like ashes.

"She Sounds Like a Bad Girlfriend…"

which witch?

bitchy witchy

the boy kissed a witch

which witch took the biscuit?

witches like the milk in first

the witch loved another

the witch told a lie

bitch

witch bitch

she's so twisted

a demon's apprentice

she'd have her cake and eat it

witches take their sweet time

the witch cursed your name

the witch faked a smile

bitch

drive her round the twist

her eyebrows don't match

she sounds like a bad girlfriend

the witch and the drama kid

she didn't love you

which witch?

the witch faked a lot of things

bitch

Becoming

sometimes I let the minerals dance
upon each taste bud before
I swallow them down, like magic

~

it makes you fear the mundane:
the floorboard creaks and the deafening
volume of a room far too quiet.

~

night-time shadows like to waver
figures of hesitation, apparitions
but not quite ghosts. something other.

~

what do you do once the magic
has gone down, settled in your gut
to manifest like an illness

~

it keeps you awake at night
you toss and you turn like something
is brewing in the pit of your being

~

I have lost count of the moments
I feel it; a lily bud blooming into a

perfect image of death.

~

I sleep very little. moonlight treasures
are too precious to miss— I drink in
potions like I used to sip my coffee.

~

it always comes to me early, when
the mortals are dull and absent. I
wake to the sound of a sleeping world.

~

my world to craft. a caricature of
our haven of magic. aglow with a
delicate sheen of moonlight.

~

kiss my sugared lips until
they are red and raw, suck
the poison out until you glow too.

~

come and meet my midnight
firelight, shaped like an archetype
illuminated with a delicate amber glow

~

the end becomes beginning as

the moonlight fades its shine
and the witches take their time.

~

they paddleboard along the rivers
and leave their sorcery on poetry
pages, an unknown enchantment

~

a new age; dull the fires and throw
embers to the dust—

no caricatures to sketch from the charcoal.
no treasures lost beneath the river faces.
no ragdoll bodies suspended in these forests.

Oracle

January 16th
It is the night before her hanging—
unconfirmed officially, but she knows.

The witch is haunted by a peculiar ghost,
lurking in shadows, reflecting in mirrors;
he grins like a devil. Ever present. The witch
finds herself tormented and unsettled.

Reflections in the looking glass behave like apparitions.
As they shine in the sparkle of daylight, the witch
reflects on herself; she pictures herself a ghost or
a mortal – which will she be once the transition is done?

There is a loneliness in mortality, in the knowing
that invisible strings can both draw us together
and pull us apart.

And as the sun is set to rise, the witch is void
of this devilish tie; she wears her necklace
of rope with pride. Such titles removed,
she begins a new life.

Acknowledgements

With so much love and thanks to Dr. Jack McGowan for supervising this project. Love also to Ruth Stacey for lending me her collection of witch books and for letting me care for them throughout the pandemic.

Early versions of these poems appeared in the following publications, to which I am so grateful for the opportunity of being published alongside some truly stunning writers:

Your Tinder Match is a Witch, Dear Reader

Paddleboards, Nymphs Magazine

Snow Queen, Eremite Poetry

And thanks also to all those who let me gush about witches until the coffee went cold.

About the Author

Chloe Hanks is an emerging poet from Worcestershire. With the desire to absolve female villains from the patriarchal lens, her writing destabilizes stereotypes and reinvents what is familiar. Her work has appeared in a number of anthologies, including the recent debut from Fawn Press, and she was the winner of the V Press Prize for Poetry in 2020. She is currently studying an MA in Creative Writing at the University of Birmingham.

About the Publisher

We believe stories matter. They will be here long after we are gone.

Sunday Mornings at the River prints poetry books and helps authors realise their publishing dreams. Our aim is to create a thriving literary community where we focus on healthy and inclusive collaborations.

We believe a poet's job is much like what Salman Rushdie wrote in his novel The Satanic Verses: a poet's work is to name the unnamable, to point at frauds, to take sides, start arguments, shape the world and stop it from going to sleep. This is the kind of poetry we are looking for and publish.
Equality and inclusivity are the magical words at our headquarters (which is an old wooden dining table with too many coffee rings on it). The only power we believe in is people power. We believe that everyone has the right to be heard, especially the people that are pushed into the shadows by the traditional publishing world. We try to amplify their voices by providing a platform, and building a community, both online and offline.

We pride ourselves in being an independent and inclusive publisher.

Poetry by Chloe Hanks
@c.l.hanks
clhankspoetry.bigcartel.com

Designed, edited and published by
Rebecca Rijsdijk for
Sunday Mornings at the River
sundaymorningsattheriver.com
@sundaymorningsattheriver

Cover image
by Carl Spitzweg

Printed in Great Britain
by Amazon

86465781R00027